UP CLOSE & PERSONAL PUBLISHING

through the lens of

CATASTROPHIC
CLARITY

a poetic journey by
SANDO HAMILTON

ISBN: 9780997186437

Book Design by: JannaGeary.com
All photos property of: Up Close & Personal Publishing

Publishing Contact: Upcpublishing@gmail.com
Author Contact: Sandohamilton@gmail.com

This book is dedicated to my children and their legacy. May my words always serve as an invitation to the lens of my time on Earth.

From these pages I hope you find the depths of my spirit. I pray your journey never parallels the pit falls of its darkest content and it exceeds, a thousand times, the rejoice found in its voice.

Love you deeply, beyond the boundaries of time.
~ Dad

CONTENTS

FOREWORD

Knowing Sando Hamilton has added several dimensions to my own life. We have known one another for over 30 years and it happens as it often happens in situations, I was a guidance counselor and he was one on my counselees. We didn't have a lot in common, he was from the inner city and I wasn't. He is a first-generation college graduate and I am 3rd generation. But as I met him in my counseling office 30 years ago I found him to be a very intelligent informed person.

Sando is a student of inner-city urban life, he studies it well. This book of poems reflects much of what I am saying. He writes what he observes, he is able to observe what he sees. He has learned that he is not responsible for the tragedies of urban life but has become an astute observer of it.

Through this book he analyzes the successes, failures, and contributing factors of the Black experience along with showcasing forces which made it what it is and keeps it as it is. He enjoys trying to get you to see the world the way he sees it as he tries to show areas of hope and improvement in a situation where it lies despite knowing most people have given up on its potential. His poems reflect this, his poems on the prison pipeline in the inner city is moving, while at the same time highlights his creative ingenuity to paint vivid pictures and tell complete stories through this genre.

Sando's refusal to give up on the inner city by presenting their case to us in his writings shows an optimism which I noticed 30 years ago when I met him. He believes that everything and everybody has a point of view that's worthy of presentation.

Sando is an important voice in 21st century Black life and Black philosophy because unlike most people who write about the urban world and who has never been in it or lived it, he is from that world and has lived in it. He wants to show the reader, the stark color of what living a Black life actually means. This book is a powerful voice for those who may feel unheard and a guiding light for those that are looking to see. It is clear, concise, and driven.

-Dr. Wallace Peace

INTRODUCTION

The purpose of this book is to invite you into the world of the Black American male experience. I recognize this style of poetry may not be what people are accustomed to reading, but I think poets' job is to give a voice to the voiceless and to challenge themselves to paint the world through words, even those parts we may want to ignore. In doing so, they create dialogue, hold mirrors up so people can take a look...even when the glass is cracked and shattered. This is where the beauty of the craft comes into play. This is where the healing and understanding take place.

Every generation needs scribes to capture the social political atmosphere of their time. To serve as ambassadors of humanity and reflectors of truth, even when it reveals sides of society that are not desirable.

The poems selected in this work are told through a lens that has taken over 20 years to be published. In essence they are a part of the social conscious of the United States that started with slavery and evolved into the 1990s through the year of 2019. Their universal appeal outside of that time spectrum is only further testimony to the relevance of their value.

The goal in this work is to allow the reader a chance to experience the world through the Catastrophic Lens of Black males in the United States. To give insight to our various levels of complexities: our hopes, dreams, successes, failures, contradictions, contrast, love, evolution, and our spirituality. Whereas this book (nor any) can never speak for an entire group, it can serve as a resource for gaining an understanding to the majority and how we're shaped by the United States experience.

As an Observer of life and as a gate keeper of living history, it is my hope that you receive the words as open and honest observations even if they are not your experiences and you disagree. I made an attempt to give background information on poems to help enhance your experience and level of understanding.

Last, the spiritual piece was truly a journey. If you want to hear what the conversation was like between the Creator and I, I invite you to listen to Pat Metheny's "To The End of the World" while reading "Color Blind." The level of honesty and commitment to receive what was given back to me through the Creator is presented as I received it as a conduit of the Creator's words. I understand many may question or disagree with what is said and the rawness of the dialogue, but that is what made the whole journey of the piece so amazing. I asked and I received. Whether or not you believe it to be true is for you to decide. Regardless, I'm at peace.

Welcome to my world, I hope your lenses find clarity.
~ Sando Hamilton

PART I
THE
AWAKENING

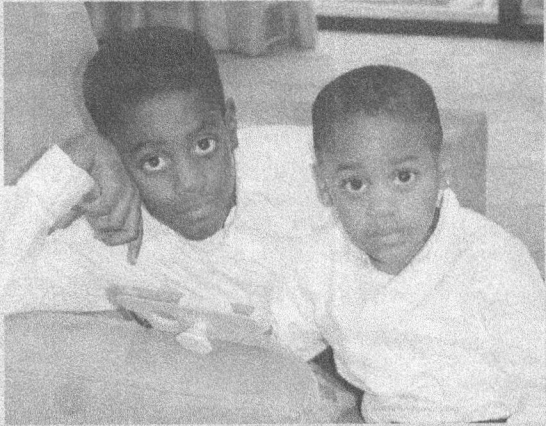

1

REFLECTION

BACKGROUND

This was the first poem I ever wrote. The year was 1992 and a dear friend was going through a rough time. The conversation was intense and centered around their state of mind in that moment, which was filled with melancholy and self-pity. In an

Have you ever stared so deep into the mirror
that you saw yourself?

Not, of course, the physical reflection that's given off when light hits its surface. I'm speaking of looking so deep that you were able to see your true self, or in other words…see your soul.

Did you like what you saw?
Did you look and see yourself cowering in a corner…
too scared to look back?

Or, were your eyes met with a distant yet piercing light that seemed to stare back and say, "I see you, you see me, and we agree…there's a mutual respect."

Hello me, I'm glad to know you.

effort to pull them from doom and gloom, I spoke the words that are now the poem verbatim. The rest is history. In life there will be peaks and valleys, they're all a part of the human experience. If you don't learn to love yourself, nothing else really matters.

2

CASUALTIES

BACKGROUND

This poem was birthed from a college lecture that involved the professor discussing European colonization and just how intimately detailed it was structured. It was the first time I ever heard a Caucasian professor speak so candidly and matter-of-fact about the atrocities of wars on nations of color. The focus was how European nations were on the verge of going to war with

# of WAR

(Berlin Conference of 1884 - 1885)

one another over the continent of Africa's resources. Instead of war, cooler heads prevailed and they decided to have a meeting in Berlin, Germany. The outcome kept Europeans from killing one another and instead allowed them to agree to split the continent of Africa amongst themselves, with each country agreeing to control the people and resources of their agreed upon area.

Meetings of stealth in Berlin required *RSVP*

Everyone who was anyone was there…with the exception of people who looked like me

They called it a *Conference*. We called it a *Nightmare*

Democracy was the code name attached to the undeclared war on the people known as *The Alpha*

Mercenaries armed with *Christ Bombs* begin to infiltrate enemy lines

"We Come In Peace" was the fight song, and it was played over…and over…and over…until eventually – they convinced themselves

To weaken the opposition, Mortar Mines filled with Willie Lynch viruses were laid to explode on any signs of aggression from the oppressed

"Divide and Conquer" was the mission statement… and it was carried out with pinpoint accuracy

BACKGROUND cont.

The poem is filled with historical allusion with a play on words that are associated with freedom and democracy. If the reader does a little bit of research on the italicized references, not only will you get a valuable history lesson, you too may discover the big picture connection on how systemic and devised the plan really was and continues to be. Rewrite the text so the dirt can't be traced.

Capitalist Business Soldiers were taught early how to be effective in controlling their oppressed assets:

Make em lame

Keep them tamed

Change their names

Control their brains

Break their spirits to keep them in place and when they pray to their god…teach them to see your face

Build institutions that promote the White race

Rewrite the text so the dirt can't be traced.

Each VIP clearly understood: "These are the keys to remaining the dominant race."

You must never allow the oppressed to truly know or love themselves. Keep *Anglo* philosophy at their center's core…and the African Assets will ALWAYS remain: **CASUALTIES OF WAR**

NOTES: I laugh when I reflect on how, another professor that was teaching a class on how to write poetry, wrote that the poem was "Propagandistic." That note continues to serve as food for thought when I work with students. It taught me first-hand that teachers and professors don't know everything and that just because you don't know something or it's out of your comfort zone, doesn't mean it's not true, its simply means you too need to pick up a book and practice what you preach…READ.

3 THEM & THEY

BACKGROUND

This poem came from a conversation I had with my mother. During our talk I kept mentioning "Them" and "They" as if they were some visible oppressor that was-seemingly-keeping people down. Yet, my mother -in true mother fashion- was not having it and kept asking me, almost sarcastically, who "Them" and They" were because in her mind it seemed as if I was making an

"Shhh. Be Quiet."

Why?
"Here They come."

Who's They?
"You know... Them."

Them and They don't exist, they're just
figments of your imagination.

excuse for not being willing to get out of my own head and push
through whatever the obstacle was I was faced with at the moment.
Determined to not be shut down and seen as an "excuse
maker" as well as in true "WTO" son form, I decided to give
my mother something to think about to see if she still felt
that "Them" and "They" did not really exist. You be the judge.

"Although inner city youth are sporting semiautomatics and military style weapons nowadays the way my uncles sported Stacy Adams."

Don't worry about it, it's just the latest fashion wave.

"And even though HIV is on the decline in the White heterosexual community and on the rise in minority communities."

Don't worry that's only because minorities have more unprotected sex than Whites.

"The fact that every strong outspoken leader from the Black community that tried to educate their people towards self-reliance has been ostracized or brutally murdered."

Don't let that bother you, they were only isolated incidents.

"With the biggest investment for many major corporations being new prisons - which happen to house more minorities than whites and just happens to create a cheaper (slave) labor force for bigger capital gains."

Pay that no mind, that's only because everyone knows minorities have a violent gene that makes them quicker to commit a crime.

You see: "Them and They really don't exist, they're just figments of my

IMAGINATION!!!!""

4

HOLLER

Where Shall I begin?

I'm told being too Black is the ultimate sin
And it makes me wanna HOLLER

Coming from the outside it would pose no threat,
but coming from the inside shows lack of respect
-for self-
And it makes me wanna HOLLER

For 4-67 you were denied knowledge of self
Never knowing that knowledge of your history meant
having true wealth

BACKGROUND

As an educator I've worked with students from a variety of
backgrounds. Each group comes with its own dynamics and
set of challenges. Early in my career I worked in predominately
African American settings, teaching literature and history. As a
person that has always wanted to know about my history, even
its ugly sides, I found it to be disheartening when students

Too many died for you to have access to books
You now have the resources and you don't even look
They would tell you about the $5 Indians
and how your land was stole

They would point out how reverse discrimination
laws are the new game being sold

How Whites are going to Black Colleges
on the minority card

Yet your inability to find value in this content leaves
me emotionally scarred

And it makes me wanna HOLLER

were openly contemptuous about things that directly impacts their lives. Through this poem, I am reminded that ignorance of the law doesn't negate you still being held responsible for knowing the rules or how it impacts you. Like the law, we study history to avoid continuously falling into its biting pitfalls. By ignoring it, you simply open yourself up for hard knock lessons.

5

PAPER REVOLUTIONARIES

BACKGROUND

As I've grown older I've come to value different kinds of personalities. I recognize not everyone can be a leader nor will everyone be a follower. In essence, it takes all kinds of people working together to accomplish a goal. However, at the time of this poem in 1998, I was growing extremely tired of people talking about problems that existed in the community. They would do a masterful job of

Milk-crate warriors:
They come as dread-lock Rastafarians
Biblical historians
Quoting words of Black soldiers of the past

Paper Revolutionaries be:
Stirring up the masses while providing no direction
Quoting biblical scripts while waiting for resurrection
In the mean time…Brothas and Sistas keep dying from lack of protection

getting people all riled up, but in the end they would fade into the background without having done much of anything except ran their mouths. Where I'm from, that's called being a "Perpetrator." I was raised to believe that "Doers Do and Talkers Talk." Which one are you? A wise person once said, "Don't talk about it BE about it. If you can't, get out the way and let the people that CAN come through."

You can't fight a revolution from the side-line

and

You can't win a revolution with
the dumb leading the blind

What good is conversation without
mobilization?
If freedom could be won through simplistic
oral stimulation…
there would be no need for us to have this
conversation…
because Lord knows we've talked about it

It is time

The Negro Revolution must come to an end
The Black Revolution in America has yet to
begin
If you've yet to understand see: "Message To
The Grassroots," that's Malcolm, Chapter 10

Stable U.S economy is not synonymous
for free Negroes

If you still don't understand see:
James Bird and Amadou Diallo

Black ancestors gave their lives for lessons not
learned

They will not have died in vain if today the
revolution begins

but if all we do is talk…
Against their names we have sinned

It is time

Stop stirring up the masses and offering
no direction

Quoting biblical scripts won't bring
His resurrection

Get in the closet and learn to keep *The Man*
guessing

and

Brothas and Sistas will stop dying
from lack of protection

6

questions.

BACKGROUND

No one can tell you what it's like to walk in the shoes of someone else. For instance, I will never know what it feels like to be gay, but I can try to understand their journey through having empathy. Empathy is merely having the ability to figuratively put yourself in someone else's shoes and try to find a way to understand the world through their lens. For the most part, this seems to be a skill that's not lost on people. However, when it comes to the Black male experiences in America many people seem to lose the ability to apply empathy. In fact, they seem to think we're full of excuses and that the playing field has ALWAYS been even, or it has been even long enough that we should all be able to simply shake off the remnants of years of systemic oppression and bounce back like ALL is well with the world.

Don't get me wrong, I'm most certainly not a person that believes in living by excuses, but I'm also not one that believes that *Post Traumatic Stress Disorder* is not real and that it can't have serious physiological and psychological impacts on its victims for years. Since most can't afford therapy, don't know where to begin to get it even if they could, or they are completely unaware they are victims of trauma and are simply going through the day-to-day motions of trying to find some form of normalcy...Black Males in America are still trying to figure out what the hell happened.

In the beginning there was darkness filled with serenity,
Next came the *light* that would forever
seal my fate…birth.

Believe it or not, there was a time, not long ago, when the President of this great nation actually opened the flood gates for additional lab rat Nazi Eugenic type research to be conducted on Black males by referencing to bogus scientific research that hinted that we might actually be born with a "violent gene." He didn't focus on his inability to give youth options for employment which led to high gang-related drug violence or that his version of creating jobs was centered around more fast-food restaurants bringing minimum wage jobs to urban areas. Instead, he played the scapegoat card and blamed the victims.

This poem is my attempt to bring some clarity to our mindset. I invite the reader to read it as if they are sitting somewhere with everything peaceful around them and in the next instance a bomb goes off and all you can see is chaos happening around you. Yet in the midst of the chaos you can see everything unfolding in front of you in slow motion with crystal clear clarity. In doing so, I invite you to see the world through the lens of many Black males in America…through catastrophic clarity. The goal is not to get sympathy but to, at the very least, tap into your empathy.

(Turn the page)

How does it feel to come into the world a member of the endangered species list?

Better yet, how does it feel to know you were added to the list the moment you were conceived in your mother's womb?

What's it like to born into a world that predetermined you to be the *bad guy*, the insignificant guy, the we *don't give a fuck* guy... and never bothered to ask for your consent?

The Illuminati got your mind so confused you sometimes begin to think you did this shit to yourself.

How does it feel to go to school and have your parents told about the learning disability you somehow miraculously developed once you started school?

And if they're not convinced, reinforcements are sent, in the form of that school psychiatrist, who casually recommends *Ritalin* to calm down that hyperactivity that was once viewed as being young and energetic, but is now rewarded with
Learning How to Become a Dope Fiend 101.

How does it feel to know at the ripe age of sixteen you are expected to be prepared to graduate into the prison system so free labor and Capitalism can live on?

Big Brother got you so caught up in your day-to-day survival, you can never focus on the big picture to see who your real enemy is.

How does it feel to know *if* you graduate being able to add, read, and write…you are the exception, not the rule. But, if you walk away functionally illiterate…that's what was expected, so you're cool?

What's it like to go to school to learn to become someone you're not? I'm told - if you learn your lesson well…you can come out and beg for a job through affirmative action?

How does it feel?

What does it feel like?

Who would know the answers to such frustrating questions?

7

liquid drapping

BACKGROUND

This poem is the namesake of a play that was written and performed by students from a mentor program I started. The purpose of the group was to use data from reading scores to identify at risk males entering 6th grade and then create a structured support system that would foster a nurturing environment to strengthen their education outlook academically, socially, and emotionally. Needless-to-say, the

36

"a b c d e f g

As soon as I'm 9 I begin to see…"

program had great success. Once empowered, the youth wanted to tell their story and decided to present a play about the pipeline to prison and how the journey begins long before someone is actually physically locked-up. They were shocked to see it begins as early as the age of nine (if not sooner) in schools across America that often begin labeling Black and Latino students, especially males,

My head begins to swirl
as my world goes in a twirl of a constant spin

I'm looking for the pause button,
reaching for the pause button,

but this picture seems to have no end

BACKGROUND cont.

as maladjusted during their elementary years. This is not to say
that some students are not really SERIOUS problems in classrooms
across the country. But where some see a problem, I often see
lack of innovation, close-minded thinking, and failure to adjust to
what's really important to young people to build around their focus.

I'm suddenly tossed into an abyss world of
darkness with cold steel tables and lurking
shadows called: *The Land of Dark Men*

Forgive me Father for I seem to have sinned

What did I do to get handed this fate?

What will it take to get back on track
to keep my life straight?

In this world money seems to rule,
in this world no one seems to care about school,
In this world when you drop-out…
You graduate…so that's cool

This poem tells a story of the on-going struggle for Black and
Latino males to escape the remnants of slavery while still being
systemically targeted to remain victims of free labor, also known as
the industrial prison complex or slavery 2019. It walks you through
where the journey often starts and sadly where for many it ends.

Refusing to accept this path I choose to fight

But "Resistance is futile" I'm told…so just deal
with the plight

Learn to live with the urban blight

Learn to always remember: you're wrong and
they're Right

It's written in the laws so it as simple as
Black and White

Hopefully you'll get mad and want to fight

Go grab your crew and do something stupid
out of spite

BACKGROUND cont.

Note: I think it's important to point out that I don't have a problem with inmates paying their debts back to society by working it off productively, but if an inmate proves to be a great worker in prison and they work hard for the .12 - .40 an hour they're paid working in the 2 billion dollar federal prisoner mandatory

This way they can control you and have you
humbly bending to their might

Recycle you in and out of the system like
changing wheels on a bike

Retract on your voice to vote while kissing
goodbye to your civil rights

YOU learning to read was never a part
of the plan

So they kept it basic and taught it in a way
you couldn't understand

This was their way of creating the
NEW and *Improved*
Intellectually Inferior BLACK MAN

work programs. I also think when that person is released, if
they desire or need a job, they should be allowed to apply to
work for that same company making a real world sustainable
income. The mere fact that this is not an option, only further
feeds the notion that the system is not designed to rehabilitate,
it's designed to cultivate a cycle that's hard to break free from.

One who comes fully equipped with big bully
brawn and no brain

Who, by 16, has been systemically broken,
mentally choking, and therefore easy to train

One who has come to hate himself
so much he's struggles to maintain

Passes his self-hatred on to his seeds for
generations so they can taste, drink,
and live his pain

Now you're making excuses on how you can't
read and write because you got caught up
in the *game*

Can't get or keep a job because you're last
in the food chain

Labeled as Functionally Illiterate
and written off in the government's budget
as a societal strain

If you don't start fighting for your survival...
you'll disappear like a stain

This is real talk, so it comes without malice,
spite, or disdain

Either take heed of the warning signs
or you'll get left by the train

"a b c d e f g
As soon as I'm 9 I begin to
see..."

8

NIGHT MARE

BACKGROUND

This poem was written before the political shake-up of 2008. I placed it in the book as a reminder of the frustrations that many minorities felt before Michelle and Barack Obama arrived on the national political landscape. It was born in the classroom when I was trying to get a group of urban high school students to

Last night I cried…as beautiful Black boys
bragged and made bold bodacious statements
about getting high

It pained me to see they were too caught up in
the Matrix to realize their reason of
justification was nothing more than a
pre-programmed alibi

So slick and hip to the *game* they were …the
didn't realize they were *game* set free to be
caught up in the *game* by the *real* game players

And…

Last night I tried…to explain to the young sista
that asked me, "Why does it always have to be
about race?" that I wasn't the one who devised a
plan to steal the soul of man and recreate him

engage in the lesson. They seemed disconnected from the value
of the lesson and instead found more happiness in discussing
how they had partied and got high the previous night. Whenever
and wherever I encounter young people that have this kind of
outlook, for me it is, it was, and will ALWAYS be a nightmare.

in the image of me. "You see, I'm simply a casualty from a distant land searching for ways to get free."

And...

Last night I lied...to my child when she looked at me with youthful excitement in her eyes as I came to realize she could never strive to be President of her nation: America the Free, Home of the Brave, Land of the greedy made rich by the slave.

And, realistically, her faith would probably be spent trying to keep the government from putting her back on the plantation

You see there's a game being played and the stakes are high, if you live you win but if you lose you die, tag muthafucka tag...you it, die muthafucka die that's it. I'm seeing visions of destruction that's being born within, I'm fighting devils with no faces and they're starting to win

I feel like a doctor that walks into a room of destruction that says, "Damn, If I had only got here a second earlier."

So...

Last night I pried open damp depressive doors (with no regards for self) trying to save unborn minds from being trapped behind burning collapsing floors as they...pulled out their Sunday's best preparing for daily sermons to be delivered from neighborhood heroes known as pimps, players and whores. Who was once seen as man's lowest profession and has now been ordained to hear his confessions

So...

You see there's a game being played and the stakes are high, if you live you win but if you lose you die, tag muthafucka tag...you it, die muthafucka die that's it.

I'm seeing visions of destruction that's being born within, I'm fighting devils with no faces and they're starting to win

9

teacher ballad

BACKGROUND

I reflect back on a time, during my teenage years, when in my hurry to prove that I was grown, my mother posted a sign on the refrigerator that read as follows: "Teenagers: Tired of being harassed by your parents? Act now!!! Move out, Get a Job, Pay your own way, While you still know EVERYTHING!!" -Author Unknown-

"Teacher Teacher" I'm smarter than you

I can run the class and do what you do

"Teacher Teacher" You ain't heard, "I'm the MAN!"

I'm going take over the world, I don't need no plan

When It comes down to this school thing "Who needs a book!"

I can take over the world simply with my charm and my looks

"Teacher Teacher" I'm going to be PAID

I guarantee I'll make a million and I won't need no grades

As an educator, I've worked with students from every level, but my greatest times have been spent working with 11 - 14 year old students. Like the teens before them, they swear that the world started the day they were born, and like the teens that will come after them, many will choose to learn the hard way that that it didn't.

What's this you say about going to college and
chasing dreams

What's this you claim about how knowledge is
POWER…that crap sounds like a scheme
"Teacher Teacher" that stuff may work for only
a few

My Brother ain't go to college
he got a brand new Benz at Twenty-two

I know you tired of singing that same ole song

That's why I'ma be the one that proves ALL
y'all wrong

"Teacher Teacher" you really think
you know it all

I ain't got to go to class or study hard as long as
I can ball

"Teacher Teacher "I got talents galore

I got so many talents I hand them out to the poor

I got a 40 inch vertical and can dunk from the free throw line

Plus, I run a 4.1 forty with 50 pound weights dragging behind

Did I happen to mention that I can also sing and dance

Or that I can fight better than Ali when given the chance

I bet you didn't know that I'm strong as a bull

These are all the things you need to have if you want to have some pull

"Teacher Teacher" why won't they let me graduate,
They holding me back for nothing and messing wit my fate
The paper says that I can't read and write or add math higher than two
"Teacher Teacher" my plan didn't work, what am I supposed to do?

10

MY BROTHA

BACKGROUND

This poem is born from a variety of personal observations and experiences. It is in essence a culmination of my much needed life's lessons at the point in my life when it was written in 1998. I continue to hold on to the valuable lesson it contains.

"He's Not Heavy, He's My Brotha," that's what they say. But sometimes, every now and again, I get a chance to look him directly in his face and for a brief moment...our souls make eye contact.

For a brief moment I see the transient enslaved being that's held in the somber darkness of his existence, or in other words I can see his soul, and try as he may, his soul reveals the hidden truths his strategic poker face has mastered to conceal.

It is in this instance that I am blinded by the *celestial light of reality* that reveals with precise clarity everything he has mastered to conceal.

For a-brief-moment, I can see images of me diving to catch him from falling from the steepest mountain as we climbed looking for hope, prosperity, and peace of mind. I see images of me leaning over a cliff hanging on to him with all my heart and inner strength, with my fist clutched so tight that small drops of blood ran between my fingers from my nails digging into my flesh.

For a-brief-moment, I see images of him falling and me picking him up to carry on my back as we attempted to cross the hottest desert to reach freedom.

Allowing myself to make grave sacrifices, and though my body was physically and mentally drained, I carried on with each step being a test of will, while allowing the desert sun to beam down on my naked back causing the skin to bubble from being cooked alive by its' blazing ultra violet rays. But it was worth the sacrifice because: "He's my Brotha...right?"

Wrong!!!

You see I now begin to comprehend the hidden truths his soul was fighting to reveal. His soul has managed to say *everything*...by simply saying *nothing*. As I looked deeper, I began to see, *"there was no mutual look of love, no signs of gratitude for my sacrifices."* As a matter of fact, the only look that was obvious is the look that said: **"What took you so long to catch me from falling?"** and **"Have we reached our destination of freedom?"**

As our souls held direct conversation...all of sudden his eyes opened wider in a stare of desperation as my forefinger slipped, as I began to recall the time when we were in school -receiving the same opportunities - and he chose to dropout to -as he put it- *handle his business.*

I could feel his heart jump when my middle finger broke its grip as I began to recall thoughts of him selling drugs to make ends meet to support his *Nike Addiction*, while poisoning his community and when asked, "Why?" his naïve stupidity told him to say, **"If I don't, somebody else will."**

His feet began to search for leverage when my ring finger fell in agony from my flooded memory of seeing him hang out on corners drinking and gambling. While in the meantime, waking up in the morning to *exist* merely for the sake of *existing*. Yet, at the same time, watching me go to work so he could *put in his work for the homies* at my expense.

Words of "Help! Brotha, help me!" began to echo out into the open sky as my pinkie finger collapsed during a flashback of when he was on top and I needed his support...only to never see it being offered. I began to recall how he wouldn't even budge because he was too busy looking out for *(Masa's) The Company's* interest.

Finally, with new insight and a look of no remorse, I casually pull away my thumb. Watching as he falls to his destiny in a twisted spiral. As he falls, our eyes meet. It is in this instance that his eyes seem to say what I have longed to hear…however, it is too late. I stand up alone, staring out into the vastness of the serene open sky, pausing momentarily to take advantage of my newly found tranquility, seizing the time to draw upon reflective thoughts to see where *I* went wrong…when suddenly I come to my conclusion: You see…"He was not my *Brotha*, just someone who happen to look like him."

The Struggle continues…

11

NIGGAZ AND BLACK FOLKS

Niggaz and Black Folks both are a joke

Niggaz and Black Folks are still being
lynched...but with different ropes

Niggaz are lynched by systematic oppression

Black Folks are being lynched
with the illusion of *acceptance*

To be a Nigga requires no education or degree

BACKGROUND

This poem represents the personification of two dividing mindsets that are prominent in the African American social and political psyche. The poem is created to hold-up a mirror for the Black community with the hopes of allowing us to take a long hard look at our differences and offer a chance to have dialogue around the

But to be Black Folks means you have
to conform to society

Niggaz swear they're down
and that they can't be faded

Black Folks think degrees make them educated

What we fail to recognize is they both
have a common bond:

Neither one has a pot to piss in and only one
leg to stand on

Until Niggaz and Black Folks can remove the
nooses from around their necks

Niggaz and Black Folks will never know the
true meaning of the word: RESPECT

strengths and weaknesses of both. Which one you choose to identify
with is entirely up to you. My only hope is that in the end, you are at
peace with what comes your way from either. Niggaz and Black Folks

12

THESE EYES

Momma once said, "The eyes are the windows to your soul."

So I started practicing keeping my eye shut at eleven years old

Not because I was scared, but because at eleven I could see the world was cold

I didn't want to freeze

BACKGROUND

With the smooth seamless departure of the 44th President, Barack Obama, administration and the torrential entrance of the 45th President, this poem was written to offer the reader a chance to experience the reality of what America was faced with when "45" entered the White House.

So I learned to look for security blankets that
would fight the chills from the breeze blowing
off the oceans of life

Seen too much too early and played dodgeball
with Strife

Learned about heroes that were gunned down
and cut up from racisms cold knife

So excuse me if I refuse to open my eyes
to take a look

But all this pain I've seen has got me shook

These eyes have seen too much

Fast forward to sixteen, where I got introduce to the maniacal world of fiends

Walking through life with soulless eyes

And when you looked deep enough you could see tattered bruises left from systematic bitter twisted lies

It didn't matter how many families were left in disarray

Sam's belly needed to be filled so your pain was simply the *"Meal of the Day"*

It came served with fresh melted *Government cheese* and *sweet canned apple juice*

For you to swallow your *hood's* sense of hopelessness as you fought to break loose

Trying to run away and not look back, but you can't run too fast when soulless eyes are on the attack

So excuse me if I refuse to open my eyes to take a look

But all this pain I've seen has got me shook

These eyes have seen too much

I can't believe it happened...
I made it to twenty-five

Not because I didn't want to, but where I'm from it was hell staying alive

You've run a strong quarter mile in the heap of life

Time to play the Official Game...you know "Get a real job, a house, a car, and a wife"

Go forward and claim your piece of the American Pie

You've invested into the System, it OWES you a try

You're a vet, a college grad...the world is YOURS

But you can't find a job and the bills are starting to rain and pour

Can't figure out why when you've done everything right

You refuse to believe it's the system smacking you out of spite

So you make NO excuses you face it like a man

You stand on your principles of righteousness and do the best that you can

You know you're qualified to get a small business loan

You send in your app and wait…no need to complain and moan

So when the letter arrives that says you were denied

Is it because you weren't trying or simply weren't qualified?

Is it because you caved in on the fight and refused to fight back?

Or is it because you were born with a disease that's called being a male that's Black?

So excuse me if I refuse to open my eyes
to take a look

But all this pain I've seen has got me shook

These eyes have seen too much

What happens to "a dream deferred?" is a
question once asked

What happens when a man's back becomes
broken even after doing his fair share of the
task?

When he asked for nothing and tried to carve
his own way

When he squeezed lemons from every drop
and sprinkled it with sugar trying to sweeten
up his day

When he's tried to turn the other cheek and
shake off the brutal punches of life's blow

When he's turned to the Good Book for guidance and asked God to show him which way to go

When he's stood up on principle and worked himself to the bone

When he's found himself abandoned feeling empty and alone

Isn't this the time when life should hand him a break?

Offer him time to recover to get his life straight

Realize he's been a soldier fighting for everything he has

Shouldn't Life wrap his feet with bandages from walking on broken dreams and glass?

Isn't it only right to finally offer this man something to not keep him in a slump?

And if your answer is "Yes" then why would we EVER elect … TRUMP

So excuse me if I refuse to open my eyes
to take a look

But all this pain I've seen has got me shook

These eyes have seen too much

13

BEWARE
OF THE
"ANTI"

Anti-this
Anti-that
Anti-gay
Anti-Black
Anti-gun
Anti-fun
Anti-God
Anti-Jew
Anti-me
Tomorrow it's...

Anti-YOU

14

RIGHTS

BACKGROUND

This poem was born out a conversation with a dear friend that has the honor of serving as a first generation politician in his community. During our conversation, he mentioned that he was sick and tired of having to fight for equal access to human rights and felt that as a Black man he was reduced to the Bronze Package of rights: Civil Rights. He went on to mention that until there is some basic accountability for holding White America accountable for respecting people's human rights, Civil Rights will forever remain the consolation prize for any and everyone that is not a White Male. This dialogue sparked further reflection about the various levels of rights as defined by history and how those rights have been distributed amongst mankind around the world since organized societies first came into existence and the poem was born.

There's a game being played, but many don't even know they're in a fight

They walk around with blinders, thinking they have equal access to rights

They say: "All men are created equal with certain inalienable rights"

But Rights haven't been equal since the word first came into the light

At the top of the pile, sits the Platinum Pack, but since these rights are divine

They were reserved for monarchs, Popes, and Pharaohs, too pricey for the un-sublime

Next up to bat is the heavy hitter in the game,

However Human Rights are reserved for members only of certain linage attached to certain names

Access to its club is what all humanity craves,

Yet access is granted on a pay-to-play basis, with veto power reserved for descendants of slaves

So what rights can one claim for self if one wants to get in the game?

One can claim Civil Rights, it's the Bronze Package deal passed out to all the lames

Though it won't put you at the table for you to feast amongst the kings

Nor will it let you claim humanity as your own when demanding equality is what you bring

It's the package that allows you to at least be thankful for their mercy when you're begging for a job, marching, and lifting your voice to sing

15 THE NECESSARY TRUTH

BACKGROUND

This poem finds its roots in the political turmoil of 2016. 45 is newly in office and the country is heavily divided. On one side of the flag leading the charge for American's right to protest unjust policies through civil disobedience are the Black Lives Matters organizers and athletes kneeling to protest police brutality towards minorities. They are joined by protestors demanding that Civil War relics be removed from public places because, like it or not, the SOUTH LOST and losers should not be held-up as American heroes in places that are paid for with public tax dollars. Especially if the side that lost was fighting to keep members on the winning side as SLAVES and the descendants of those slaves taxes are being used to maintain public images of their oppressors.

On the other side of the flag were disenfranchised Whites, being led by proud card-carrying members of the Ku Klux Klan, the Aryan Nation, and every other "anti" minority group that found its way back into the forefront when 45 came into office, seemingly, representing their collective way of thinking. Their shared desire is to "Take

Ladies and Gentlemen, welcome to battle
of the ages

It's a battle that has been building and
bubbling under our feet prophesized by
Kappernick sages

America back, by making her great again." The disenfranchised
Whites felt their way of life was being challenged and once again,
minorities were pushing too hard to gain equal access to the
American Dream by removing their version of true American heroes.
Sitting on the side lines are the lackadaisical Whites that
don't seem to feel *45* is playing a game of divisive politics
and that everything in the country is moving along just swell.

Both sides decide to march in Charleston, South Carolina,
ironically the same state where the American Civil War began,
and the contemporary *Helter Skelter* showdown begins to
brew. Unlike previous Presidents, *45*, decides to not upset his
political base by condemning their actions after one brave
young woman is killed and others are injured when a proud
White Supremist decides to drive a car into the crowd. Instead,
45 chooses to announce to the nation how "Both sides' were at
fault. Thus, setting the stage for his political arrival and forever
deeming him as the nameless President who will forever be "*45*."

The stage has been set between the so called "Left" and "The Right"

In each corner, the main combatants of this earth-shattering battle just happen to be White

No need to adjust the channel, you can no l onger hide from the spite…even if you try to run from it with all your might

For years minority voices have shouted about the wrongs of the land

And for years Whites from both sides have looked the other way while claiming they simply couldn't understand,

"What do you mean when you say there's a systemic war that's been waged against the dark skin man? That can't be true because racism is simply not a part of the American plan. That's the thinking of the Old…we're living in a new day. Racism in America…no how…no way."

So it's business as usual in the land of the free

When it's time to elect officials, no need to worry about a candidate's past or credibility

If they were accused of rape that's not really a big deal, and if they swindled business partners out of millions…that's just the way of business and how you close deals. If they got in bed with the enemy, why not, the enemy called and was willing to share? If they spew hatred and bigotry…that's just shows they really care.

Why choose a candidate that helped pass the health care bill, it makes more sense to choose a candidate that says exactly how they feel.

Plus we need a leader that can get us back on track, especially after that last one messed EVERYTHING up….the one that just happens to be Black

As a matter of fact…

I think it's time we *"Take America Back"*

"What do you mean when you say that's coded language for systemic hate? That's not coded language at all, it's all about making *America Great!* Why does everything always have to be about race? Believe it or not there's reverse discrimination happening all over the place."

Can't believe it happened, tell me it's not true!

I didn't vote for *him*, I chose not to vote at all,
what else could I do?

Think about it…according to the news…
she was crooked too

We're FINALLY back in charge, right where
we belong,

Got control of the Senate, The House, and
Oval Office with our numbers growing strong

So it's out with *Affordable Care* and up with the
wall, it's out with environmental concerns that's
allegedly good for us all

"What's wrong with doing God's will and
getting rid of gays and queers? *45* should be
celebrated for his humanity and met with
Nobel Prizes and cheers. That's not being racist,
that's being against mortal sin. If it means
kicking *them* out of the military, then that's just
where we'll begin."

No big deal If since inauguration day hate crimes have a new spark, no need to investigate a Black Muslim being hung from a tree in the park. No need for concerns regarding militia flags waving and Klan torches lighting up the dark

American history is under attack and it needs to be preserved, Geronimo, Chavez, and King got exactly what they deserved. And what about real American heroes like Lee, Davis, and Wallace that fought to preserve the rights of the Whites? These are the stories that should be passed on to our children to finally tell the story right

"What's wrong with retelling history from your point of view, if facts get left out or dropped… well that's nothing new. It's not systemic racism if I refuse to read real history books, and it's not systemic racism if I turn a blind eye to tough cops that others call crooks. If someone died by their hand, it's probably the victim's fault, and don't be claiming Black Lives Matter if some-one dies once they get caught."

"The Chickens come home to roost," are words that were once said. It got the person that said them banned because a President ended up dead.

Yet these words still carry weight…just like they once did, they remain a reflection in the mirror when the Left and Right finally pull back that lid

What they'll find is what's always been there… the monster of hatred and racism spreading its stench into the air

So now you've felt its sting when a car was driven into a crowd, as hateful words were being spewed with Nazi and Klan members marching strong and proud

While *Heather Hyer* laid there dying stretched out in the street, where the *Left* and the *Right* in Charlottesville finally came to meet.

Where the reality of America's temper showed its ugly face, where the bigotry predicted by the sages is now claiming its own race

And when you turned to *45* in hopes of words to heal from the grief, he gave you what you voted for and offered no relief

So here you now stand with the monster staring you in the face, are you going to keep turning a blind eye and letting its stench permeate the space?

Bigotry, Hate, and Racism is not a child's game or spoof,

Sadly, Heather's death is just another claimed victim of its proof

You can choose to go back to your world where you ignore reality and move about aloof

But for the minorities of America the question now becomes...

What will White America do now that they have witnessed a Necessary Truth?

16

MANHOOD 101

(Dedicated to the men who shaped me.
Inspired by my Brother Walter 1/15/2019)

BACKGROUND

There are a lot of versions of what it means to be a man. Some base their definition on age, some on a rites-of-passage, some on a series of actions that must be completed, even if those actions, at best are rooted in pseudo warped versions of manhood like having sex, drinking and smoking for the first time, getting hair on your private parts, or even robbing/killing someone as a gang initiation.

I grew-up with manhood being presented as a series of definitive actions and deeds that matched expectations at certain ages. My taught version came along with physical, social, and spiritual obligations that were required to be met and the word man culminated into an acronym with nation being the foundation of the word.

As it was taught to me: The core of every nation is family. Therefore, a man must be able to maintain his family by being physically/emotionally present. He must understand socially he has a responsibility to step up and hold others accountable when they are not carrying their load in the community. He also understands that how he carries himself socially is important because youth want to emulate what they see. Therefore trying to talk to underaged girls you watched grow-up and putting packages of dope in a kid's hands to help them take care of the family falls short of meeting the obligation. Last, a man must have something bigger than himself at the head of his life. No matter what you call it: God, Allah, Jehovah. A male who is humble to nothing is a threat to himself and others around him. All three must be met to be a Man, otherwise you are a Male working towards manhood. This is not meant to discredit anyone else's version of how they chose to arrive at what works for them. But this is my creed of manhood and how I have tried to live my life according to what I was taught.

I am thankful for the men that have been in my life and that helped cement those traits through being living examples of what they taught. They passed the baton to me and I'm glad that I can pass it on to others, I pray that I remain worthy.

Out of all my worldly possessions that I love to display

Manhood is always my choice of the day

Not because it makes me feel big and bad like I can never lose

But because in the name itself is the path of life that I choose

M is *maintain* or move mountains in all that you do,

carry yourself in a manner that represent the best parts of you

A is literal, it means exactly that,

it also means as a descendent of *Africa* I embrace being proud I'm Black

N is *nation*, the foundation of where I stand,

the source of my strength, what makes me a faithful friend,
fierce foe, and peaceful protector of my land

Maintain A Nation is in my DNA,

helps me love myself and others, stand for what
I
believe, say what I mean and live by what I say

H is *humble honesty*, always be so with self,

doing so brings peace of mind, it enhances
mental health

O's are overt and obtuse obstacles, they exist to
help you grow,

If you meet challenges head-on and rise from
falls your light will continue to glow

D is *deliberate diligence*, live by it every day,

set goals, love hard, cry deep, laugh till it hurts,
it is in your DNA

17

THE SCHOLAR'S PLEDGE

Out of the mist of darkness and into the light

I accept knowledge as my friend and welcome
ignorance with spite

I will use logic and its reasoning to separate
fiction from truth

BACKGROUND

This poem is the pledge I wrote for the young men in my mentor group to recite daily. Its purpose was to serve as their mantra. By doing so, their grades and actions reflected how it became a part of their core. Its value is self-explanatory and still relevant for anyone that considers themselves a student any place in the world.

I will never blindly accept knowledge without checking for proof

I will use history and its wisdom as my mentor and guide

I will stand against mental oppression with dignity and pride

I will meet obstacles head on and rearrange statistical facts

I will let my brain be my weapon and my actions be my bat

I will pass knowledge on to others and welcome them into the light

I will carry my Scholar's torch high so my light will remain bright

I am a Scholar

18

BEACON
OF THE
NIGHT

BACKGROUND

The people selected in this poem were chosen because, at the time of this poem, despite being in the spotlight and at the top of their careers, they chose to use their platforms to serve as an example for what they believe and to give back to others in ways that far exceeded just setting something up for tax purposes and going through the motions. I

Crowned King of the court before becoming 23

Power dunking from free throws with
the greatest of ease

Internationally known, your name's on shoes

won't mention their names because I believe history will allow you to
know them through their actions and their names will be self-evident.
I chose sports and entertainers because they are, like it or not, whom
many in the Black community pay attention to as leaders and trend
setters. If that is going to remain the norm, then I feel it's crucial
to let others know what the standard of excellence can look like.

Like another *23*, got your own set of rules

We value what you do when in the moment of the game

But it wasn't until you used your voice that raised the VALUE of your name

In the end, many will remember how you played with all you had

But the *Brotherhood* will remember you for being a loving husband and dad

For having some depth and for taking a stand

For reaching back for others and lending a hand

For investing in your city and doing it with pride

For providing quality education to help youth hit their stride

---

We value you knowing you're a part of our fight, we value you knowing you're a Beacon in the Night

---

BACKGROUND cont.

NO ONE can be forced to make the sacrifices these gentlemen have made. Each person has the right to decide for what, for whom, and when/where they will or won't stand. But it's nice to see that some people still believe that: "To whom much is given, much is expected." Way to step up! Note: I'm WELL aware there are PLENTY of others

One of the best to ever do it, you're a beast on stage

Verses can be quoted for days expressing pain, love, and rage

Played the hustle game and came out on top

Got more #1s than Elvis you can't be stopped

Rep yo block hard in ALL that you do, had to send fools Reminders…nobody's bigger than you

So Smoove in how you move, You're a BUSINESS…man

But it was watching you lead by example when Prince and the Brotherhood became REAL fans

Let it be known being an owner is the place to be
Stock shot to the moon when you manned up with B

Put games to the side and took hold of your truth

Let your pain be food for others looking for ways to heal like you

who have answered the call to step-up. I can't acknowledge you all so for the time being, your contributions will have to remain between you and those that are aware of your work. Know that whomever and wherever you are "I'm glad to know you are a part of our fight." Keep doing great things…Beacons of the night.

Loving how you empowered the voice of your pen

Exposing necessary truths of pipelines leading to locked up men

Low key with support for the cause you quietly give back

Showed strength and support as needed when your President was Black

We value you knowing you're a part of our fight, we value you knowing you're a Beacon in the Night

It's not easy being on top choosing to find your own voice

Not many would do it, but you made a conscious tough choice

Playing at the highest level, you could've easily turned blind

You could have easily, turned the channel and said how we were losing our minds

You could have easily read your stats and stayed in *your athletic lane*

You could have easily listened to the voices that said
you had nothing to gain

On the field you were elusive and quick with your feet

You kept teams guessing for ways that would lead to
defeat

Many will argue your stats only seeing you through
watching from stands

But It wasn't until you chose to kneel for others did
Brothers became real fans

Never did you waver when it was presented as the
logical choice

Never did you forget **a man who stands for nothing
has no nation or voice**

"Just Do It" stock rose when they did what was right

We value you knowing you're a part of our fight,
we value you knowing you're a Beacon in the Night

"Friendship is essential" is a part of your declaration
and creed

Many claim it as their mantra, but few really truly
believe

Naturally funny, humor's your gift to share with the world

Got men waiting 90 days and uplifting their women and girls

Spreading your wings to soar while capitalizing on your fame:

Books, Family Feud, Pageants, and more…all in your arsenal to claim

Branded a King of your craft separated you from a lot of the rest

Started highlighting businesses in the Hood letting others be blessed

Took a look in the mirror saw younger reflections of self

Recognized young men without guidance and love leads to destructive mental health

Seeing you mentor others is a prize unto itself

When you came to realize your journey's bigger than you is when you gained your true wealth

We value you knowing you're a part of our fight, we value you knowing you're a Beacon in the Night

Many have been selected, few ever answer the call

The question now becomes: "What will YOU do when you have your hands on the ball?"

When YOUR chance to shine arrives and the world is your pearl,

Will YOU stand with the people or leave them hanging to unfurl?

Will YOU see the best in others using your platform to open stuck closed doors?

Will YOU lead by example to help others knowing they can do and be more?

The Brotherhood will be proud if YOU choose to stand unified in its plight

When you do, as a person of substance and strength, you'll be valued as a Beacon of the Night.

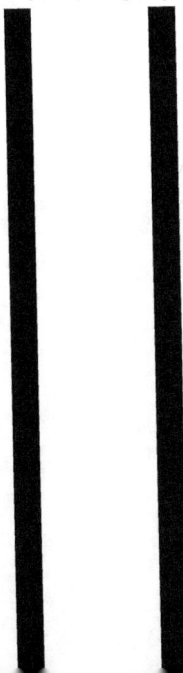

19

america.

BACKGROUND

Despite her problems, she's home and I'll defend her way of life until the end.

96

America is a gumbo pot of different races

People with different hopes and dreams from different places

It's the place that's built on the backs of slaves

It's the land of the so called "free" and home of the "brave"

Red, White, and Blue, are the colors we fly

They represent the bond that unites us when lifting our heads towards the sky

Though sometimes there's sickness that makes the country ill

We refuse to let prejudice, racism, and discrimination take away America's appeal

20

Obeezy *through* Haiku

BACKGROUND

As the First African American President of the United States, President Barack Hussein Obama kicked down the door with so much poise and class that one would have thought the door never existed. His ability to do so shifted the entire paradigm of thinking for an entire generation and potentially beyond.

This is not to say that he did not have his political flaws or setbacks, but as the first to EVER do it...DAMN was he good. He'll be thoroughly missed as our Presidential leader, but his work for social and political advocacy continues. There's really just TOO much that can be said about his tenure in office, so I decided to sum-up some key points through Haiku. Because he was also the living personification of being intelligent and cool, it would not be befitting to refer to him as merely President Obama. For the sake of his depth and versatility, he will forever be known as *"Obeezy"* to the Hip Hop Generation (Which I maintain he's a member of, despite Baby Boomers trying to selfishly claim him as one of their own. But that's a conversation for another day).

Being First takes love
You two have removed the doors
Your impact lives on

Michelle raised your cred
Choosing her showed me your smarts
The rest was easy

Beware of Lions
When they roar bad guys can die
Don't end up with fish

Through you we all shine
Black culture on world display
Royalty for Life

You Killed them with class
Head high, shoulders back, on point
What else could they say?

Hard to lead while Black
Gave too much, Gave not enough
No one knows your truth

You REPRESENTED
Last address to the nation
Done "Obama Out!"

21

farewell. my nigga

BACKGROUND

I smile deeply when I think of the journey to this poem. I was at the library doing research. The young man helping me limit my research was being extremely patient with me. It just happened to be in February, Black History month. When I looked at the bigger than life display that was filled with a variety of African Americans from several

It happened on a sunny spring day as flowers
were starting to bloom

I wanted to be there so bad

I bet it was a day filled with melancholy

People falling on the casket and having to be
restrained from being uncontrollably angry and
sad

I wonder if they gave it a dignitary's burial:
3-gun salute, Taps serenely serenading silent
mourners, the single plane breaking formation
in its final fly-by to head off into the awaiting
blue yonder.

backgrounds at the center, as usual, and bigger than everyone else
was Dr. Martin Luther King Jr. (a brilliant man, underrated strategist,
and clearly one of the most prolific public figures of his time) along
with all the normal post WWII, Harlem Renaissance, and Civil Rights
heroes/heroines.
Seeing the display seemed to bring out something in my spirit that

I imagine ALL the world news stations covered the funeral…

They had to…right?

Afterall, this was a moment that man would NEVER live to see again:

The death and final farewell of Black History.

The year was 1968, the death of Black history personified: MLK.

I wanted so desperately to be there, but sadly I was unable to attend due to not being born.

Now all I'm left with 50 years later are 28 days of celebrating him and his contemporaries: thank you McDonalds.

BACKGROUND cont.

wanted to shout at the top of my lungs: "Damn! OK WE GET IT…he was GREAT. But damn, can't someone else shine for once during Black History month? Haven't there been other contributors to the cause? And why do people seem to ONLY celebrate and highlight people

I wish I had been there to tell them not to throw time into the casket; to let it live so that others could continue to add to its rich legacy.

So that names like: Oprah, Obama, Jackson, Prince, Simmons, Jordon, Cochran, Rice, Powell, Gates, Miller, Carter, Young and countless others could come through its passage.

But I couldn't be there and no one was there to explain the value of today…so here we are, stuck in limbo with nowhere to look forward to and nowhere to grow.

A race without a present, no recollection of our immediate yesterdays, and only a collective universal memory up to 1968.

R.I.P Black History…
you could have been great.

that come from the previously mentioned time periods. Did Black History stop when Dr. King died?" And the rest, as you can now read, is history.

PART II
ARDOR, RAPTURE & WRATH

22

CLICHÉ LOVE

When the word love has worn out its meaning and
become cliché'
What can be birthed from its womb to become my
display?

Maybe space and time will become its slave
To show how you'll remain the beat of my heart until
their dying days

Perhaps it will capture the air eagles use to soar

So I can use it to find strength to breathe

when in your

absence I can breathe no more

As snowcap mountains majestically raise their crowned

heads to the sky

It will claim the trumpets of the winds howl through

their chambered doors

to forever sing our lasting lullaby

It will write love sonnets where nebulas provide cosmic
cacophonies for gravity to procreate
While painting pictures of Weaping Willows wantonly
weaping while feeding their mate

Even while trapping harmonies of wolves
seductively serenading
ornate orbs spinning in perfection
Words will never capture
the draft of our
connection

23

p & j

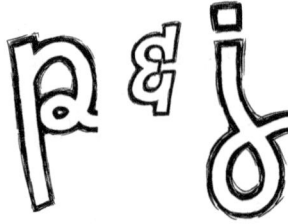

(not for the allergic)

BACKGROUND

Over the years it has been my observation that some women seem
to understand men in ways that are lost on other women. They make
men out to be more complicated than what the majority really are.
Those confused by men's simplicity are often further baffled as to why
certain things about them, that they deem as wonderful traits, are

The key to a man's heart can be found
in a peanut butter and jelly sandwich

It is essentially the sandwich of love
and how he gauges with whom he will stand

Some don't believe this to be true so they
ignore the formula's simplicity

They deem simplicity to be just that...
too simplistic...eventually wondering what happened

Overlooking what he pays attention to

Did she grab the first two pieces of bread in the loaf?

Did she find a way to make the magic
formula...complicated: imported French bread,
exotic jellies, organic natural almond butter,
with ravishing refreshing rice milk to wash it all down?

Making sure to spread each ingredient evenly so it doesn't
make a mess

Presenting it as a whole sandwich to satisfy his appetite in a
couple of bites

not viewed by men with the same vigor. This selection was originally a piece written for a friend's wedding to congratulate the bride on having found the formula. Based on the continuous high levels of confusion about the simplicity of men by some women. I feel this selection still has relevance. I chose to offer it to those that may be curious as food for thought.

or

Did she reach into the middle of the loaf, passing several pieces until she arrived at...perfection

Did she stay true to the formula: domestic white or wheat bread, Welch's Grape Jelly, Jiffy peanut butter and a glass of deliciously delightful whole milk

Making sure ingredients overlapped in such a way that peanut butter sticks to the roof of the mouth and jelly spills onto palms to be licked clean

Presenting it cut in halve diagonally or in pieces of fours for continuously having reason to make it last while enjoying the mess of every bite

He searches for who will apply the magic formula that he never could duplicate, but has spent a lifetime trying to figure out why his never quite taste the same

Reminiscing to days of school field trips with paper bag lunches, opening brown bags to discover mom's P &J. Biting into it being overloaded with taste of freshness in bread, just enough peanut butter that kept his tongue chasing its remnants while sweetness of jelly dripped. Chasing it down with milk so satisfying that all he could say was, "Ahhhh."

Coming to realize he could never duplicate the formula on his own because mom always packed the sandwich with an extra ingredient...Love

The key to a man's heart can be found in a peanut butter and jelly sandwich

It is the sandwich for which he spends his life looking for the woman who can duplicate his mother's formula of love.

LOOK AT HER

She stands with the grace of a goddess
commanding respect
without uttering a word

Her head is held high and proud as the rays
from heaven illuminates
everything around her

With her inner strength she has unselfishly
carried her nation through the years
of undeclared war on her man

BACKGROUND

This poem was written to capture the pure beauty of Black women. My motivation came from being out with some friends and having a variety of different hues, sizes, and shapes of Black women around us. Each had their own style, their own presence, their own path, but we were all enthralled and appreciative of their unequivocal beauty.

Only by permission of The Deity
can her beauty be captured

She is to be held as the most precious jewel
given since the time
when man was given a soul

You should consider yourself blessed

Look at her

Despite the hardships of their journey through slavery, education, social acceptance, and spiritual healing (just like many Black men) I wanted this poem to serve as a reminder of just how beautiful and loved they TRULY are.

OLD SOULS

In the beginning we set afloat in the abyss of space and time laughing like school children as we peaked over God's shoulder and watched him create the universe

I can remember when Heaven was our private playground and we played tag on the Rings of Saturn and swam in the Sea of Tranquility

We were two separate entities sharing the same soul, because from the beginning we were meant to be and I loved you

…then came birth

our gaze continued far beyond the norm of general eye contact. In that moment we both seemed to have been transformed back to where we met. The moment was magical, the poem captures the experience.

Cast down from our celestial perch, we were both sent to dwell amongst man, to seek answers to questions we once understood, yet we took them for granted

Facing the trials and tribulations of this world, we both searched aimlessly amongst millions... only to find ourselves feeling empty and alone

I never understood the void that seemed to
hang over my heart…until I saw your face…
until I heard your voice

Your smile spoke to my soul in a voice that
seemed familiar and I knew that once, long ago,
somewhere in the abyss of space and time…I
loved you

26

LOVE'S SACRED SONNET

If you have ever loved, been loved, want to know what true love looks and feels like…this has been my experience.

You're loved from a place with no space or time
Where stars are born, from sparkles in your eyes
Where logic's held captive, slave to sublime
Where dark matter holds planets in the sky

You're valued like water to dying trees
Through your love I've found heaven's sacred door
Without you life's a flower without bees
Your happiness is my reason to soar

You're respected with reverence and awe
A diamond shaped from obstacles of life
Perfection is birthed from your single flaw
God's gift: my friend, my love, my heart, my wife

Our love will surpass our eternal sleep
This love will remain as life's gift to keep

27

BUTTERSCOTCH ENIGMA

BACKGROUND

This poem was born from a night on the town where I met a young woman from another state that was visiting family in my area. The music at the club was good, and the lights wrapped itself around her in a way that created a hypnotizing aura. When the club ended, neither of us wanted the night to end, so we decided to continue our evening with breakfast. That's when the evening took on a new meaning.

During our conversation I got a chance to really see how intelligent the young woman was. As it turned out, she was also a Civil Rights advocate in her state, which made her even more attractive to me. We spent the rest of the evening deeply engaged in intriguing dialogue and I simply didn't want to let our time together end. It was my first and only experience of meeting someone in an instant that I knew, if she was around for longer things would have been different. Perhaps others have experienced something similar.

Hue of honey swaggered to heated hypnotic beats
Hips that hypnotized caused man-child to leave his feet
Licorice lips of lilac looked as sweet as morning dew
causes one to ponder:
"Is it your hips

lips

or

you"
Celestial cerebral told tales of ancient tranquil times
Third-eye connection under open midnight skies
Feelings of uncertainty left us feeling new
causes me to wonder:
"Is it your hips

lips

or

you"
Sirens screamed serenity so in spirited silence we lay
Holding time captive refusing to acknowledge day
Reliving stories of Eden when out of one came two
Imprinted on my heart is
Your hips
Your lips
and
YOU

28

SONNET
of
SOUNDS

BACKGROUND

There's nothing more beautifully intoxicating, or human, than the intimacy shared between two people taking their time to enjoy the moment. Enjoy

Soothing seductive sounds tell your story

They dance rhythmically uniquely to you

Like embers in my repository

Leaving lustful trails of your residue

The Melodic melodies of your moans

Pulsating pauses capturing your breath

The Heavy Heartbeat that causes you to groan

Screaming in ecstasy to escape death

Singing soprano when hitting your peak

Wantonly whispering my name in heat

Searching silently for your voice to speak

Your tantalizing tongue tasting its treat

The glee in your voice when we start to play

The life in your laugh when after we lay

29

· ·
· ·

· · · · · · · · · · · · ·

· ·

· ·

· · · · · · · · · · · ·

BACKGROUND

This poem was born from a conversation with a female friend that stated she was looking for a man that would get her pregnant and go on about his business. She didn't want to do in-vitro fertilization, she wanted a God-fearing man, with a college education to step-up and take on the task. I kept trying to explain how her proposal came across as an oxymoron and how I couldn't see a man with substance falling for it because it would contradict everything he prides about himself, but she maintained it could happen. I felt the need to capture her

· ·

· ·

donor

mindset, because I would later learn that there were a large number
of college educated women that were adopting this way of thinking
at the time. I'm not sure what led to it, or how it played out for the
children that may have come into the world through this version of
parenthood, but I hope it has dissipated.

Note: This poem was written in 1997, as of 2019 her request had not
been fulfilled.

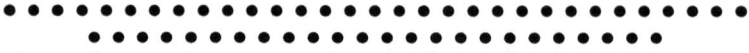

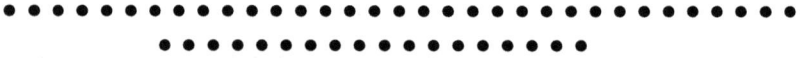

(the ad read)

WANTED:

Athletic
Attractive
Educated
Family Oriented
Good Morals
High Goals
Spiritual
Strong
Successful
and Horny
Male

to bastardize

Attractive
Educated
Family Oriented
Single
Strong
Successful
Spiritually Confused
Black Woman

30

WHO WINS

BACKGROUND

This poem is self-explanatory. I've heard stories of what some men unjustly go through in the court system and I wanted to give their plight a voice to start real dialogue. I've worked with young people as a teacher and mentor for more than half of my life and I've seen the pain that comes with the internalization of parental rejection. However, based on some of the horror stories I've heard from friends I could easily see how many men could choose to take the path of completely disassociating themselves to escape the unwanted pressure and legal shakedown the court system is actively playing a role in creating. The experience could easily leave a sour taste in a man's mouth. Is this fair, what about men? Where's their justice?

Currently: A woman can say she doesn't want a child and even if the father says he wants her to have it and agrees to sign all the needed paperwork for her to legally have the child naturally and turn all financial and day-to-day responsibility over to father with her being allowed to move on with her life, he has NO RIGHTS if she decides to terminate. On the flip side, if a man says he doesn't want any children and a woman finds a way to capture his sperm and becomes pregnant, despite his objection and her manipulation, if he's called into court and DNA proves he's the father...he's financially responsible regardless. As revealed in the poem, it actually gets deeper, but I wanted to give more background of where the courts currently stand.

This poem offers some insight to people that intentionally set out to play deceptive games without regard to how it impacts those you claim to love. I hope you receive it and grow.

Note: I am by no stretches of the imagination endorsing any parent that went into a relationship willingly and knowingly from being held accountable for their parental responsibilities. My goal is to highlight the issue around people that are intentionally lied to and manipulated against their will to be come FORCED parents.

Who wins in the end when your whole
existence is a lie?

When one parent schemed to get you here
using you as an alimony alibi

Who wins in the end when one plays
power games

While the other tries to do right, but the
games create disdain

Who wins in the end when
"I want no children" was made crystal clear

While words went completely ignored
and the other schemed to get you here

Who wins in the end when if he
innocently steps-in he's stuck

Cause the courts says, "That child needs a
Dad," since he bought shoes and food,
according to the law…he's fucked

Who wins in the end when some
use the system as a trap

Courts can't force him to love what he grew
to despise and eventually he snaps

Who wins in the end when the child
grows nourished in anger

Do the lies that were told that's fixated in
their soul lead them away from lurking danger

Who wins in the end when they refuse
to be involved

Did you have this in mind as you plotted
and connived thinking your victim
would eventually evolve

Who wins in the end when the baby years are
gone, you're struggling along, when the streets
start calling your child's name

Did you think cause they share blood the plot
would lead to love with him gladly
giving his last name

You failed to think

You created this stink the moment
you played your game

Who wins in the end?

31

young love ballad

BACKGROUND

Something to ponder. How would you have handled this?

The story of young love

they say it's from above

Cupid's fitting like a glove

Got you thinking it's for life

Beyond today, tomorrow, in the afterlife

Dreams of being man and wife

then comes the knife

that cuts deep and leaves strife

You constantly can't keep from calling

You really don't know what to do

You're in a freefall falling

Your emotions are starting to brew

You're begging for forgiveness

You're trying to start anew

You're struggling to catch your breath

What are you going to do?

Two weeks has passed since it ended

You've started to amend

You're back to being yourself

You're looking for new friends

You can breathe and walk outside

No longer wanting it to all end

You spot them with someone else

They look just like your twin

You constantly can't keep from calling

You really don't know what to do

You're in a freefall falling

Your emotions are starting to brew

You're begging for forgiveness

You're trying to start anew

You're struggling to catch your breath

What are you going to do?

You're second guessing their words

Playing them over in your head

Wondering if **ANYTHING** was ever **REAL**

Did they mean any of what was said?

Feeling cheated, heated, and defeated

You decide you want revenge

How can you make them suffer?

How can you start to win?

Head stays in a spin

You devise a clever plan

They'll pay for their sin

You organize with your clan

Catch them alone, have an alibi

Watch their every move from afar

Somebody has got to die

"We loved one another,"

Is found on the note telling "Why"

You constantly couldn't keep from calling

You really didn't know what to do

You were in a freefall falling

Your emotions continued to brew

You begged for forgiveness

You tried to start anew

You struggled to catch your breath

What else could you really do?

PART III
AGAPE LOVE

32

FATE

BACKGROUND

This poem was written to personify fate. None of us can escape our destiny…even if we try. Therefore, don't be afraid to take chances, tell the ones you love, adore, and admire how you feel while you have time to do so. Time is not promised, eventually we will all dance with Fate.

Fate awakes each morning with a smile on its face
and a mission on its mind
"Just *gotta* take the first step out of that
comfort zone,
because we aren't promised a whole lot of time"
is what many like to hold on to
But Fate likes to tap them on the shoulders
and deliver gifts of irony with sprinkles of
twisted intertwined destiny...
which is the substance of things hoped for
All it takes is just the size of a mustard seed
So Fate has become the gardener of us all
Spraying its nutrients on each of us
Wrapping us firmly in the awaiting arms of Time
and
Watching from the Fields of Possibilities
as we begin to blossom
into ripe fruit that's ready to be harvested

33

JOHN'S LENS

(We Honor You: Humbly, Graciously,
and Thankfully)

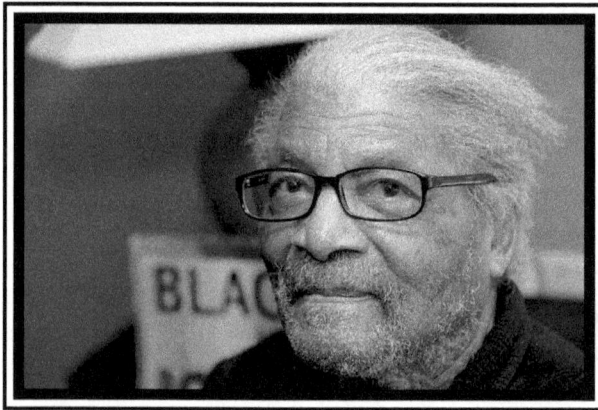

BACKGROUND

This poem was written to honor Brother John H. Williams, the visual historian of Omega Psi Phi Fraternity Incorporated. For more than 60 years Brother Williams used his camera to tell the story of one of the Black community's royal jewels: Omega. Through his historic contributions, generations will gain insight into the limitless

boundaries of their potential while paying homage to many of the pioneers on whose shoulders they stand. He lived to be 100 and was called home February of 2019. I pray my words live to honor him forever more.

Many people have vision, but they fail to see past the
mist of darkness into the benevolent brilliance and
powerful essence of our fraternal Black Sea
Their minds remain clouded by murky swamps created
by main stream society
Failing to rise out of the night that covers us all into
the daylight of our regality

But Not John, he was given the gift of clarity that
captured the beauty of our living history

He made time his muse and painted the world
through spectrums of light,
Made us all see ourselves differently through his
images of black and white
Added our Black beauty to the rainbow's hue lifting
us from the murk and the blight

Through John's lens we gained perspective and learned
the value of celebrating ourselves
We saw our Manhood put on public display
Scholarship saluted in every way
Prevailed through Perseverance with no delay
All while continuously Uplifting ourselves and others
each and everyday

Through John's lens sons learned that life
ain't been no crystal stair
But If you could master your dreams by seeing it
through you could rise beyond her wear and tear
You could build bridges for others to cross
mountains with no excuses blanketed from despair

Through John's lens our history will continue to speak
Even beyond this place of wraith and tears, when at
Omega's old gold gate we meet
Where royal purple aligns to welcome Brothers
who are thy own gripping when they greet
Calling out into the heavens how Friendship remains
Essential to the Soul and Friendship we will
forever seek

34

Mountain men

(For my Brothers)

BACKGROUND

Every year I spend quite a bit of time in the mountains with some of
the most humble, balanced, knowledgeable, and beautiful spirited
men that a person could ever meet. They have served as my mentors,
my guides, my friends, and my brothers. This selection was written

during one of our departing ceremonies. I believe it serves as a
reminder of our bond, respect. and love for one another.

Memories are reflections

Reflections are moments held captive by time

In them we find the essence of all that makes life dear

In them we find lost treasures that have been washed over by new stimuli,

but held captive as precious jewels that we simply can't afford to lose

In them we find rays of light that act as beacons on our darkest nights

that lift us from the canvas after being knocked down in the fight

that nourish our spirits to overcome plight

that help us find the strength to push forward and strike back with might

Reflections/Memories are the threads that hold us together...remember to NEVER let them go, for in doing so you lose the essentials fibers of you

Let the sounds represent life, allow the sounds of the drums to be the heartbeat...hear the rhythms of life in its echo

Let the sounds of hands clapping be the sounds of celebration, rejoice, and thankful reverberance of the lives that have touched our own and have left their presence embedded on our spirits

Let the shakaree be the sounds of harmony and balance that interweaves in and out of our daily lives as we seek to maintain life's groove beyond earthly pain and spiritual uncertainty

Let the loud bellowing of our silence be our screams

our remorse

our reflections

our love

our healing

our acceptance

our thanks

35

THE INNATE ENEMY B.K.A CURIOSITY

Running, running, running, with nowhere to hide

Trying to keep my sanity because I'm losing my mind

BACKGROUND

This poem is the beginning of the spiritual portion of the book. It offers you a chance to know more about my mindset and how I grew-up being taught to be an independent thinker. Believe it or not, sometimes it's the gift and the curse.

The Questions keep coming back to
taunt me

My logic keeps popping up to haunt me

And because I can't hide from myself,
I'm lost in the reality

How do I escape the claws
of the beast called "Curiosity"?

It keeps me from being able
to live in peace with my sanity

The deity said, "Don't question me" and
"Just believe," yet he made me innately
curious about things I cannot conceive

This has left me in a state of disarray

seeking answers to questions that will
be only be answered during *Judgement*
if there is such a day

The following three selections will take you on my journey into
my arriving at peace of mind. They are not written to influence or
persuade anyone, they are merely a revelation of my journey.

36

Heaven
and
Hell

People often speak of the words "reincarnation" or "Déjà vu" as if they have been on Earth before yet in a different body. I too have had this kind of experience. There is something that lays deep inside of me, in the pit of my inner spirit, that tells me I've been here before. Based on the way certain strategic things come so easily to me, I feel as if perhaps in another lifetime I may have been a great soldier or tactician. It's because of these feelings, along with the Heaven and Hell concept that I come to the following theory:

Perhaps we've all been here before. Perhaps Earth, as we know it, is just a testing ground to see if you can pass the test to enter Heaven (or in other words: "gain freedom"). If this is actually true, then perhaps Earth is Hell.

Before totally dismissing this theory as being absurd, let's examine some of the outstanding traits man exemplifies on Earth that could lead to seeing Earth in such a manner: On Earth there is famine, murder, disease, pain, suffering, hatred, and war...which, in my opinion, are ALL things that can be attributed to Hell.

I know some would argue that these are the direct results of Adam and Eve eating from the tree of knowledge, but perhaps that theory needs further clarity as well. Perhaps when God decided he was going to kick Adam and Eve of the Garden of Eden, maybe (based on the description of Eden) Eden was Heaven. So when God decided he would kick them out and they would know pain, suffering, death, etc... he was actually condemning them to Earth (or in other words "Hell").

Perhaps we experience such thoughts of reincarnation or Déjà vu because each time we are born on this planet we spend a short lifetime (our lives are short when measured on the spectrum of time) trying to earn our way back into Heaven/The Garden of Eden. And, until we learn to fix the mistakes that were made in our previous lifetime, we are continuously being reborn/reincarnated.

Perhaps when Adam and Eve were created they were not created in a physical form. Perhaps they were created truly in the image of God, which is not physical…God is spiritual. Perhaps when God grew angry with them and they were condemned to Earth/Hell they were then trapped in a shell of physical containment (or in other words "the human body"- which is designed to be able to experience the different sensations God wanted man to experience as a lesson).

Perhaps (especially if you believe in the Trinity) when the Bible speaks of Jesus being born to Mary and coming to Earth to save man, that was nothing more than God in the physical form to see how man was doing in our quest to regain his favor. According to the Bible… we failed. As a result of this failure we are still trapped in this physical shell/the human body being reborn/reincarnated learning to get it right and earn our way back into The Garden of Eden/Heaven in the true image of God…spiritual.

Perhaps those who are fortunate to get it right are no longer trapped in a physical form. You see man because of physical captivity is limited to Earth/Hell. However, those that have been set free are now able to roam the galaxy to explore the true meaning of the word "existence" not just "life". You see "life" is a shallow word when compared to the time frame of the word "existence": to "live" is short, but to "exist" is eternal.

Perhaps when man builds satellites and sends them to other planets exploring to see if there is life beyond Earth, maybe life is not found by man because the life that exists is beyond man's senses. You see all of man's senses are designed to detect things on a physical scale. Therefore, perhaps the life that exists is spiritual and truly free to exist without being disturbed.

37

Color blind

Child: Father forgive me for I have sinned, I've also discovered my vision has been acting up again.

Father: You say you sinned my child, tell me what it is you've done, for surely as your father I can find forgiveness for you as my son

Child: I've gone against your teachings and walked between the lines, I've found loop holes in your words that have left me color blind.

Father: Color blind you say, how can this be, for am I not the God of man that created the land, the air, and the sea?

Child: It is true Father that is truly what you are, but the question now becomes are you also the God that created the largest known star?

Father: What is this you are asking me and how has this thought came to be, as my child and humble servant do you not believe that I am what I have said to be?

Child: My questions are not about doubt Father, my questions are about getting to know you, for as my father I can't say that's something that you've really allowed your children to do.

Father: How can you say that my child, how can you speak that as your claim, have you not heard me in your thoughts whenever you spoke my name?

Child: It is very true Father, whenever I've called on you there's been answered call, but these are not the kind of things that have kept me pondering at all.

Father: So tell me what my son, what is it you want to know, as your father I am here to guide you and help you grow?

Child: The questions I seek are not ones you may want to hear, they are questions that have left many of your children trembling with fear.

Father: And there my child is mistake number one, for ONLY truth can be revealed through me, The master of all things The Earth, The Moon, and the Sun.

Child: Well if you are ready for my questions, I'll go ahead and begin, but remember Father I come to you as your humble servant allegedly created because of sin

I'm curious about you and from where you came, I'm curious if you have parents, and if so what's their name.

I want to know if you're a child that has an active imagination, or if being an engineer and architect is merely just your occupation?

Do you have down time and if so what do you do? Are you a large living creature and does our universe exist inside of you?

These are some of my many questions just to name a few.

Father: I see you are a thinker and this discussion can be nice, but before I really reveal all of this you might want to think twice.

Regardless to if I have parents I am the ONLY God you shall know, I am the God that has set the time into motion of when you are born and when you will go.

It is true I am a designer, engineer, and architectural creator of life, it is also true that I am a destroyer that will cut you down with strife.

All of your existence resides inside of me...from the farthest reaching stars to your largest roaring sea; Your level of understanding of existence is limited to only me...therefore I am the God to you that I have always claimed to be

Child: I'm thankful Father that you have set the tone of our talk, it gives me comfort to know you are responding without mock.

Your responses have opened-up the door for me to move closer to the line so that I may point out to you how I've become color blind.

Father: Then I'm glad my child you have received me well, please continue to speak and I'll continue to tell.

Child: So many questions, I struggle with where to begin, I guess there's no better place to start than this thing called sin.

I've been taught you sent rules to help govern our life, yet in my opinion those rules have created a whole lot of strife.

You said man shall not kill even though you created war, you said man shall not covet what another man has yet you've allowed many to go hungry and others to be poor.

You said man shall not steal, but what if it's to survive. Do you honestly expect someone to abide by those rules when they're fighting to stay alive?

How can we worship only you when you have so many names? And why do your various names cause man to fight, kill, or behave insane?

You state we shall honor our mother and father, but if they don't honor you? What if they are abusers and cruel then what is a child to do? Shall they take the abuse quietly because that's the plot of their life or shall they find a way to protect themselves even if it's with a gun or a knife?

You don't want adultery to occur, so I guess this means your mate controls your every ember and fire. But what if your mate has become sick or ill and no longer has physical desire? What if they simply have chosen to abstain from your touch because of the stresses from life, if they aren't supporting your needs are they still considered to be your husband or wife? Where is the rule that addresses this concern and why is the only rule in place is that if we sin we burn?

Father: Your questions are intriguing I can see how your vision has started to blur, but you have to understand I am complex and there's a reason why all these things occur.

I gave man sin not because I wanted to keep you narrow and straight, I gave you sin so you wouldn't stray too far away and begin to lose your faith.

It is true that sin can have an impact on your eternal wealth, but it's no different than one cigarette having a long-lasting impact on your health.

I know who and what you are for I designed you as so…but it's because I know who and what you are that I have left room for you to grow.

Sin is in place to help give you lines that I prefer you don't cross, but I also take into consideration circumstances that may lead you towards protecting yourself from pain, suffering, and serious loss.

One sin does not determine the debt of your fate, but one times a 1000 begins to become great, if you find yourself committing the same dangerous offence, do you not feel it's only right for punishment to commence? After all, life has been given so that you can learn, and hell-fire has been lit so that your infidelities will burn.

Do not mistake me my child for being foolish or dense....I am the God of life that has created common sense.

I would not expect you to stand idly by and just lay down your life, and I would expect you to protect yourself from a bad parent even if it meant using a gun or a knife. I would expect if you're hungry for you to do the best you can, and if it meant stealing to survive than I'll take a look at your fellow man, for if he had food and he left you to die, then your burden will become his for failing to help you try. And if all has been given to you and you have only found ways to be a con...then my judgement will be just when it's time for you to move on.

Adultery is tricky and it's a very thin line, but people find ways to abuse power, they've been doing it since I introduce them to time. It's easy for one to sit back and say what one wants to be, it's another thing to carry the burden to live up to the creed. A sick husband or wife has opened the door for a reasonable shift from the norm and a negligent husband or wife has created just cause for one to move on. You choosing to stay also comes with a price, but that is something I have left to be discussed between each man and his wife.

Child: Your response has brought me clarity and I'm beginning to see, perhaps I'm not really as blind as I thought myself to be

There are still other questions I would like to know and I am thankful to you Father for allowing me to grow.

Father: Seek and you shall find my child that's my claim to fame, for remember I am God your master I will always answer when you call upon my name.

Child: Then let's continue our dialogue, there's more I want to know, so far you've been open and honest about helping me to grow.

Father I can only go off what I've been taught and the things that I've read, so please don't take offence to what's about to be said.

Father: You've come to me humble and I can see what's in your heart, continue to speak your truth and I'll continue to do my part.

Child: According to the books Father, there are a million stories being written and told, some seem to borrow from other groups that allegedly was not in your fold.

Father: Not in my fold….how can this possibly be true, for am I not the God of ALL man from the ancient to the brand new?

Child: I say not in your fold Father for they did not call you by your name, they referred to you in different tongues and ways and their worship of you was not the same. They looked towards the Sun and they recognized it as you, they even called the name of different gods and claimed them as you too. There's more to add to this Father, this has definitely impacted my sight, because I've been told that some have left their bodies and visited you where there's no light, there's speak of past lives, being judged and sent back, there's speak of people worshipping trees and animals for giving them food and shelter on their back.

How can this be Father and what will you really do, will you really destroy these people for calling you by a different name and honoring you the way they do? Or will they feel the scorn of your wrath by being wiped from the face of the Earth and have to start anew?

Father: I see how this concern may cause mental strain, but like you my child I'm known by many names.

It is true some like to claim me as their own, but I cannot be contained by a ballot or a thrown.

As my creation, you must know many like to claim themselves to be a parent's favorite child.

However, I am the father of all your existence and that is not my style.

Am I not the father of all animals that live in the air, the land, and the sea, which also means they too have the rights to claim themselves as a part of me.

To try to contain me to one's self is a sign of an insecure child, and they only do so to make others feel they are at the top of the pile.

I value all of my creations equally my son, as the father of all life this is how it is done.

Child: Thank you Father for helping me to see, but if you do not claim one group over another why would you allow one group to claim themselves as carrying your legacy.

They take parts of you and make it their own, they state you have given them dominion over the earth and Heaven is strictly their home.

They claim that to know you one must only come through them, their claims have caused chaos and destruction worldwide and left only mayhem.

Are you giving them rights to represent themselves as your agents of truth or will there be a price to pay for overstepping boundaries and being uncouth?

Father: The fact is my child it really comes down to the purpose being presented when man speaks from his heart, if his words are helping man do right by others I won't tear them apart.

Yet if in his heart he carries only ill will, if he uses my spirit to justify his thrills and to kill, then when I choose to snatch him from man's arms he will surely pay his bill.

Man needs guidance and I know this to be true, for without guidance, there would be no me or no you.

Child: What do you mean Father when you say no you, for you are ALL of existence and all we know to be true

Father: It is true my child all of your existence resides in me, but without your presence and gratitude which of my creations captures the essence of the sea

I have given you the ability to paint and to sing, I have allowed you to soar through the sky like a bird with wings.

I have given you feet to dance and rejoice, as well as ears that are in tune with my voice.

I have anointed your hands to build and to write for without you capturing my essence I would not exist through words or deep insight.

Man are my eyes that I use to examine what I build, you are my vessel I use on Earth and I am your shield.

Child: You say on Earth Father, are you saying there's other life forms that exist, have you also created thoughts of existence that man somehow has missed

We know there are other planets that orbit in space, but they don't register with life signs that will support the human-race.

From what man has been able to find, the earth is your masterpiece and everything else is below the standard's line.

The other planets are great for blocking objects that float through space with serious girth, but if they can't support life what's really their worth?

I'm not asking these things to show disrespect, Father I'm really asking these things so you can help me connect.

Father: There's energy in your words that you don't understand, like when I was shaping existence and my thoughts created man.

Your words show me you are still a mere child, for your thought process registered as juvenile.

Throughout our discussion, I have listened with open ears, and now you reached a point that has revealed the depth of your fears.

I can see why it's important to you to think that you are at the center of it all, your statements have left me amazed and shows simple arrogance and gall.

You actually feel because YOU can't sense

something it doesn't exist, YOU really feel because you can't see life all around you it's something you missed?

I am GOD of all existence, I have created perfect bliss.

The life around you is running its course, it knows nothing of you and has its own source.

Though I am GOD to ALL and things come through me, when I created existence all things were not created for you to see.

There is life around you my child like oxygen fills the air and just because you can't detect it doesn't mean it's not there.

They exist in harmony to learn and grow just like you, they too have obstacles to overcome and have to start anew, they too have curiosities of me the way that you do.

But to think you're alone in existence is such a small thought, know as the God of ALL existence I determine which battles shall be fought.

There are battles being fought that you can't conceive and there are things that exist that you simply aren't designed to receive.

Child: Then how is this fair Father, why would you limit us as such, why would you lock us in prison, this is too much?

You claim knowledge is power yet you won't let us grow, you claim you are ALL of existence but that's only because that's ALL you show.

Are you afraid to let us really grow because you're afraid we'll become as powerful as you, is this the reason for your denial and why you do what you do?

Are you protecting your own interest and you really feel fear, do you feel if we grew too large you would be left alone here?

With no one to bow before you and state claims of you being great, is keeping man limited really keeping us from our fate?!

Father: I

Child: You state you are the Father yet you limit your seeds, you like us dumb and subservient and not able to read.

If I was a god I would never hold my children back, I would give them what they need, there's nothing they would lack.

They would be the best parts of me and I would set them free, this is what being a GOD is really supposed to be!

Being a GOD is not all about keeping your children down…being a GOD means you have earned the right to claim that crown!

Father: AM

Child: Have you limited us Father because you see us as entertainment, or a joke?

If we didn't write you into existence would your voice have gone un-spoke?

Or would your presence have failed to be something we seek?

Would we still glorify the way you take advantage of your children by keeping us meek?

Is Heaven for real or does it exist only in our mind?

Will we really reunite with our loved ones and become a part of existence when we escape the boundaries of time?

Father: YOUR

Child: Are the books of faith filled with real stories of truth, or are they myths being passed on to give us something to argue and something to do?

I'm sick of being blind, walking in the darkness unable to see, I'm sick of chasing my tail searching for pieces of me!

I challenge you Father to let me grow, I challenge you Father to show all of what you KNOW!

Father:GOOOOOOOOODDDDDD!!!!!!

Father: As my child I have created you to push yourself to grow, but remember I am your father and you will never know ALL of what I know

If I gave you the answers to all the questions you seek, you still would not find peace in the many languages I speak.

You are designed to seek answers to force yourself to grow, there would only be death for you in my world, where would be left for you to go?

You exist to learn from life and experience as much as you can, but remember you are designed with the limitation that come along with being man.

Is your goal to become me and give birth to worlds, even if it means you will fail to exist as man and your existence would unfurl?

When the time comes and you no longer exist in this form, I will reveal to you the next level of existence that will become your new norm.

There too you will have limits on what you'll be able to know, and there too I will exist to help you grow.

As your father I give you room to show me what's inside of your spirit and at your core, and what I see is what makes me to take things away or decide to give you more.

The fact that you seek answers and want to know me is what I want of you, and it is because you seek answers humbly that I give you the room to grow that I do.

Your questions reveal you are not afraid to speak, as my humble servant I will always guide you towards answers to help you find balance in what you seek.

Do not mistake my willingness to receive your thoughts as me being meek. I am your father, your God, there will always be parts of me that will remain mystique.

Child: As your humble servant Father I want to thank you for all you've done, for your gift of life…for air, the oceans, and the sun.

For giving me a chance to speak openly and for hearing me out, for answering my questions with such clarity that you removed my ability to have doubt.

I know in my heart-of-hearts that you are real, I know in my heart-of-hearts that it's your presence that I feel.

I know I will live my remaining days as a reflection of your word, and I know I will serve you in the next life and will never waver or become deterred.

I thank you Father for having patience with me and giving me your time, I thank you Father for showing me the color in your light so that I am no longer Color Blind.

38

(famous poet)

BACKGROUND

This poem was written as a result of one of my college professors giving the class HIS interpretation of what one of the literary greats meant to say. Despite, others trying to chime in to offer their interpretation of the work, the professor seemed determined that he had the ONLY valid interpretation. I found it to be funny that he felt he could tell the class what a dead writer from 100 plus years meant to

I'll be a famous poet when I die

My words will live on as some of the greatest words

ever written in the history of syntactic expression

My "fifteen minutes of fame" will have finally arrived...fifteen minutes too late

No longer a threat to social injustice, my thoughts will be interpreted by the world's greatest
scholars so people will *finally* understand what I *meant* to say

I'll finally be worthy of an audience filled with open minds

I'll be a famous poet when I die, so until then...

I'll just sit back and

Wait

say. It also became the natural ending for this book. I don't know what
you received from my words, but I hope they sparked a thought and
left you mentally challenged or at the very least gave you a chance to
experience things from a different perspective. Who knows maybe
one day my words just might make it to a broader audience and
people will finally understand just what I meant to say as well.

ABOUT THE AUTHOR

Sando Hamilton is an American scholar, educator, and historian from the Midwest. He holds degrees in history, English, and leadership. The focus of his writing is to bring awareness to topics that often go unvoiced and to spark dialogue amongst his audience that creates opportunities for change when and where needed. This is the first release of his collective work of poetry but stay tuned for more to come.

Contact: Sandohamilton@gmail.com

www.ingramcontent.com/pod-product-compliance
Lightning Source LLC
Chambersburg PA
CBHW060050100426
42742CB00014B/2761